Sound Advice on

Microphone Techniques

by Bill Gibson

236 Georgia Street, Suite 100
Vallejo, CA 94590
(707) 554-1935

©2002 Bill Gibson

Publisher: Mike Lawson
Art Director: Stephen Ramirez; Editor: Patrick Runkle

Cover image courtesy Midas.

ProAudio Press is an imprint of artistpro.com, LLC
236 Georgia Street, Suite 100
Vallejo, CA 94590
(707) 554-1935

Also from ProMusic Press
Music Copyright for the New Millennium
The Mellotron Book
Electronic Music Pioneers

Also from EMBooks
The Independent Working Musician
Making the Ultimate Demo, 2nd Ed.
Remix: The Electronic Music Explosion
Making Music with Your Computer, 2nd Ed.
Anatomy of a Home Studio
The EM Guide to the Roland VS-880

Also from MixBooks
The AudioPro Home Recording Course, Volumes I, II, and III
The Art of Mixing: A Visual Guide to Recording, Engineering, and Production
The Mixing Engineer's Handbook
The Mastering Engineer's Handbook
Music Publishing: The Real Road to Music Business Success, Rev. and Exp. 5th Ed.
How to Run a Recording Session
The Professional Musician's Internet Guide
The Songwriters Guide to Collaboration, Rev. and Exp. 2nd Ed.
Critical Listening and Auditory Perception
Modular Digital Multitracks: The Power User's Guide, Rev. Ed.
Professional Microphone Techniques
Sound for Picture, 2nd Ed.
Music Producers, 2nd Ed.
Live Sound Reinforcement
Professional Sound Reinforcement Techniques
Creative Music Production: Joe Meek's Bold Techniques

Printed in Auburn Hills, MI
ISBN 1-931140-27-8

Contents

Sound Advice on Microphone Techniques

Microphones: Our Primary Tools

The study of microphones is a lifelong quest. For our purposes, we must understand some basic principles, techniques and terminology in order to function in the recording industry. Each mic offers a creative tonal color for your audio palette. Whereas you might struggle to get the perfect sound using one specific mic, simply changing to a different mic could yield excellent results. If you study the material in this book, you'll begin to understand microphones with a new creative, artistic and technical insight.

The microphone is your primary tool in the chain from sound source to audio storage medium. There's much more to mic choice than finding a trusted manufacturer that you can stick with. There's much more to mic placement than simply putting the mic close to the sound source. The difference between mediocre audio recordings and exemplary audio recordings is quite often defined by the choice and placement of microphones.

Using a mic to capture sound is not as simple as just selecting the best mic. Once the mic is selected there are two critically important factors involved in capturing sound using a microphone:

- Where we place the mic in relation to the sound source

- The acoustical environment in which we choose to record the sound source

Although there are hundreds of different microphones available from a lot of manufacturers, they essentially all fit into three basic categories: condenser, moving-coil and ribbon. Condenser and moving-coil mics are the most common of these three, although all types of mics can be used creatively in recording as well as live situations.

Condenser Microphones

Condenser microphones are the most accurate. They respond to fast attacks and transients more precisely than other types, and they typically add the least amount of tonal coloration. The large vocal mics used in professional recording studios are usually examples of condenser mics. Condenser mics also come in much smaller sizes and interesting shapes.

Use a condenser microphone whenever you want to accurately capture the true sound of a voice or instrument. Condensers are almost always preferred when recording: acoustic guitar, acoustic piano, vocals, real brass, real strings, woodwinds, percussion, and acoustic room ambience.

Condenser microphones (especially in omni configuration) typically capture a broader range of frequencies from a greater distance than the other mic types. In other words, you don't need to be as close to the sound source to get a full sound. This trait of condenser microphones is a great advantage in the recording studio because it enables us to record a full sound while still including some of the natural ambience in a room. The further the mic is from the sound source, the more influential the ambience is on the recorded sound.

Phantom Power

The capsule of a condenser microphone requires power to charge the metal-coated membrane. Power is also required to amplify the signal from the capsule up to microphone level.

It's a technical fact that each condenser microphone needs power to operate. The source of power for a condenser mic (called phantom power) can come from a power supply in the mixer that sends power up the mic cable, from an external phantom power supply or from a battery within the mic. If you use batteries to power a condenser mic, always be sure the batteries are fresh and that they're supplying sufficient voltage to optimally run the microphone's circuitry. Phantom power is the best way to supply power to a condenser microphone because it's constant and predictable.

Phantom power is sent to the microphone from the mixer or external phantom power supply through the mic cable. There is little electrical danger to the user since phantom power is low voltage and very low amperage DC current. In addition, phantom power has no adverse effect on the audio signal being carried by the mic cable.

Moving-coil Mics

Moving-coil mics are the standard choice for most live situations, but they are also very useful in the studio.

Moving-coil mics are the most durable of all the mic types. They also withstand the most volume before they distort within their own circuitry.

A moving-coil mic typically colors a sound more than a condenser mic. This coloration usually falls in the frequency range between about 5kHz and 10kHz. As long as we realize that this coloration is present, we can use it to our advantage. This frequency range can add clarity, presence and understandability to many vocal and instrumental sounds.

Moving-coil mics have a thin sound when they are more than about a foot from the sound source. They're usually used in close-mic applications, with the mic placed anywhere from less than an inch from the sound source up to about 12 inches from the sound source.

Since moving-coil mics can withstand a lot of volume, they're ideal for close-mic applications. Since they add high-frequency edge, and sound full in close proximity to the sound source, they're good choices for miking electric guitar speaker cabinets, bass drum, snare drum, toms or any loud instrument that must cut through the mix. Use them when you want to capture lots of sound with lots of edge from a close distance and aren't as concerned about subtle nuance and literal accuracy of the original waveform.

Moving-coils are typically used in live performances for vocals since they work well in close miking situations, add high-frequency clarity and are very durable.

Ribbon Mics

Ribbon mics are the most fragile of all the mic types. This one factor makes them less useful in a live sound reinforcement application, even though ribbon mics produced within the last 10 or 15 years are much more durable than the older classic ribbon mics.

These mics are like moving-coil mics in that they color the sound source by adding a high-frequency edge, and they generally have a thin sound when used in a distant miking setup. When used as a close-mic, ribbon microphones can have a full sound that is often described as being warmer and smoother than a moving-coil.

Pickup/Polar Patterns

Cardioid

Most microphones have what is called a cardioid pickup pattern. This is also called a unidirectional or heart-shaped pickup pattern. The unidirectional mic is most sensitive (hears the best) at the part of the mic that you sing into. It is least sensitive (hears the worst) at the side opposite the part you sing into. The

Cardioid Pickup Pattern

A microphone with a cardioid pick-up pattern hears sound best from the front and actively rejects sounds from behind. With its heart-shaped pickup pattern, you can point the mic toward the sound you want to record and away from the sound you don't want to record.

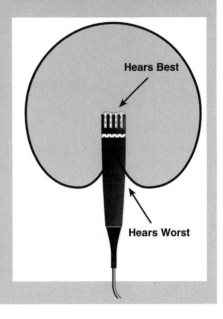

advantage to using a microphone with a cardioid pickup pattern lies in the ability to isolate sounds. You can point the mic at one instrument while you're pointing it away from another instrument. The disadvantage to a cardioid pickup pattern is that it will typically only give you a full sound from a close proximity to the sound source. Once you're a foot or two away from the sound source a cardioid pickup pattern produces a very thin-sounding rendition of the sound you're miking.

In a live sound setting, cardioid mics are almost always best because they produce far less feedback than any other pickup pattern.

We should be familiar with two other basic pickup patterns: omnidirectional and bidirectional.

Omnidirectional

An omnidirectional mic hears equally from all directions. It doesn't reject sound from anywhere. An omnidirectional pickup pattern will give you the fullest sound from a distance. Omni microphones are very good at capturing room ambience, recording groups of instruments that you can gather around one mic and capturing a vocal performance while still letting the acoustics of the room interact with the sound of the voice.

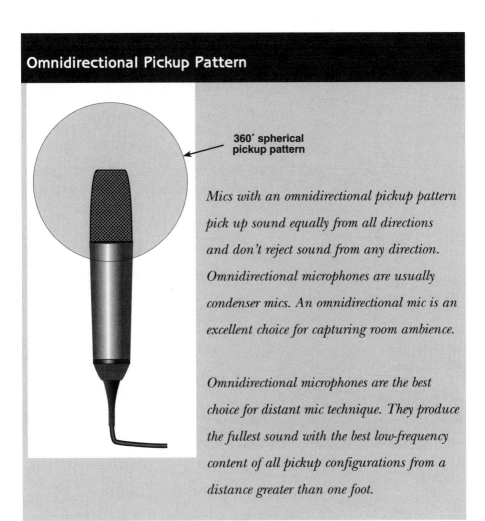

Omnidirectional Pickup Pattern

360° spherical pickup pattern

Mics with an omnidirectional pickup pattern pick up sound equally from all directions and don't reject sound from any direction. Omnidirectional microphones are usually condenser mics. An omnidirectional mic is an excellent choice for capturing room ambience.

Omnidirectional microphones are the best choice for distant mic technique. They produce the fullest sound with the best low-frequency content of all pickup configurations from a distance greater than one foot.

Omnidirectional microphones are usually difficult in a live setting because they produce feedback more quickly than any other pickup pattern.

Bidirectional

Bidirectional microphones hear equally from the sides, but they don't hear from the edges. Bidirectional microphones are an excellent choice for recording two sound sources to one track with the most intimacy and least adverse phase interaction and room sound. Position the mic between the sound sources for the best blend. Once you've committed the sound to one tape track, there's not much you can do to fix a bad balance or blend.

Frequency Response Curve

Almost any microphone responds to all frequencies we can hear plus frequencies above and below what we can hear. The human ear has a typical frequency response range of about 20Hz to 20kHz. Some folks have high-frequency hearing loss so they might not hear sound waves all the way up to 20kHz, and some small children might be able to hear sounds well above 20kHz.

Bidirectional Pickup Pattern

Bidirectional microphones hear equally well from both sides, but they don't pick up sound from the edge. This is also called a figure-eight pattern. Bidirectional mics work very well for recording two voices or instruments to one track.

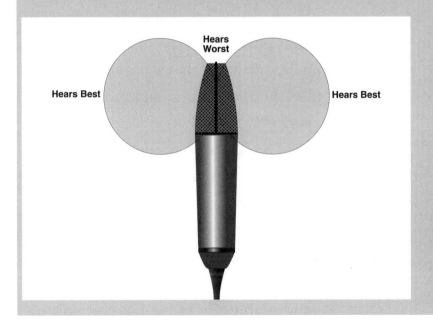

For a manufacturer to tell us that their microphone has a frequency range of 20Hz to 20kHz tells us absolutely nothing until they tell us how the mic responds throughout that frequency range. A mic might respond very well to 500Hz, yet it might not respond very well at all to frequencies above about 10kHz. If that were the case, the sound we captured to tape with that mic would be severely colored.

We use a frequency response curve to indicate exactly how a specific microphone responds to the frequencies across the audible spectrum. If a frequency response curve shows a peak at 5kHz, we can expect that the mic will color the sound in the highs, likely producing a sound that has a little more aggressive sound than if a mic with a flat response was used. If the frequency response curve shows the low-frequencies dropping off sharply below 300Hz we can expect the mic to sound thin in the low end unless we move it close to the sound source to proportionally increase the lows.

The frequency response curve is one of the most valuable tools to help us predict how a mic will sound. What the frequency response curve doesn't tell us is how the

Sound Advice on Microphone Techniques

Frequency Response Curves

A mic with a flat frequency response adds very little coloration to the sound it picks up. Many condenser microphones have a flat, or nearly flat, frequency response. This characteristic, combined with the fact that they respond very well to transients, makes condenser mics very accurate.

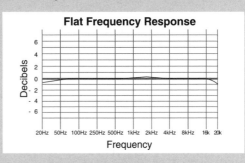

The mic represented by the curve below isn't very good at recording low-frequencies and it produces an abundance of signal at about 4kHz. Though this mic wouldn't be very accurate, we could intelligently use a mic like this if we wanted to record a sound with a brutal presence. Many moving-coil microphones have this kind of frequency response curve. Moving closer to the mic helps fill out the low frequencies.

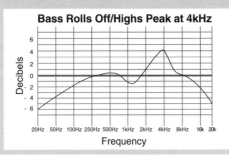

mic responds to transients. We can predict the transient response of a mic based on what we already know about the basic operating principles of the different mic types.

Stereo Mic Techniques

Much of the stereo imagery that's included in your recording starts with fundamental mic technique during the initial tracking. In order to achieve depth, acoustical interest and space in the initial recordings, good mic technique is a must.

X-Y Configuration

Let's examine a few of the standard stereo miking configurations. Each one of these techniques is field-tested and has proven functional and effective. Listen very carefully and analytically to these examples.

In Audio Example 1, listen very closely to the sound of each ingredient of the stereo recording. Listen to the position and timbral change in the sounds as they move around the room.

Audio Example 1

X-Y Configuration

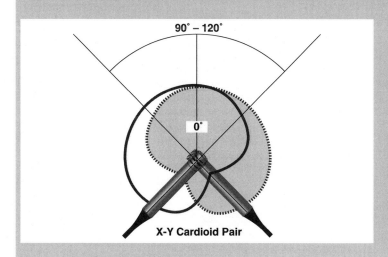

X-Y Configuration

This is the most common stereo miking configuration. The fact that the microphone capsules are as close to the same horizontal and vertical axis as possible gives this configuration good stereo separation and imaging while also providing reliable summing to mono.

90° – 120°

0°

X-Y Cardioid Pair

Spaced Omni Pair

Two omnidirectional mics spaced between three and ten feet apart can produce a very good stereo image with good natural acoustic involvement. When recording a small group, like a vocal quartet, keep the mics about three feet apart; for larger groups increase the distance between the microphones. Use this technique only if the room has a good sound.

Spaced Omni Pair

The ambience of the recording environment will color the sound of the recording. "D," on the diagram, represents the distance from the center of the sound source to its outer edge.

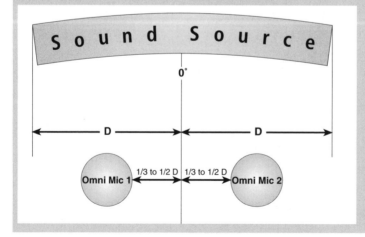

A variation of the spaced omni pair of mics involves positioning a baffle between the two mics, which increases the stereo separation and widens the image. Notice, in Audio Example 3, how clearly defined the changes are as the percussion instruments move closer to and farther away from the mics.

Crossed Bidirectional (Blumlein)

The crossed bidirectional configuration uses two bidirectional mics positioned along the same vertical axis and aimed 90° apart along the horizontal axis. This is similar to the X-Y configuration in that it transfers well to mono, but the room plays a bigger part in the tonal character of the recording.

MS Technique

The MS technique is the most involved of the techniques we'll cover, but it's the best in terms of combining stereo to mono; it also gives a very true and reliable stereo

Crossed Bidirectional (Blumlein) Configuration

The crossed bidirectional configuration isn't significantly degraded when the stereo pair is combined to mono. The sound produced by this technique is similar in separation to the X-Y configuration with a bit more acoustical life.

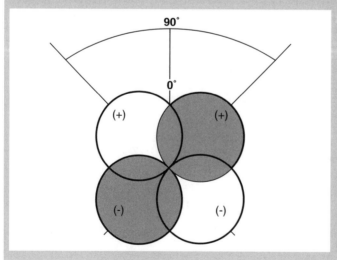

image. Most stereo mics contain two condenser capsules that are positioned in an MS configuration.

To understand how the MS configuration works, first realize that M stands for "mid" and S stands for "side." The mid mic is aimed at the middle of the stereo image and can possess a cardioid or omni polar pattern. The side mic is bidirectional and is aimed to the sides.

The mid mic is sent equally to left and right. The side mic is also sent equally to left and right but the phase is inverted 180° on either the left or the right side. In stereo, the result of this configuration sounds very similar to the X-Y configuration and results in a very good stereo image. In mono, because the side mic is reversed in phase between left and right, the side information is canceled; that leaves the mid mic as if it were the only mic used. In other words, there's absolutely no phase problem when the stereo image is summed to mono.

Listen to Audio Example 5 to hear this stereo mic configuration in action.

Audio Example 5

MS Configuration

These microphone configurations are very important when trying to achieve good, natural stereo imaging. Keep in mind that the acoustical environment

MS (Mid-Side) Configuration

To minimize negative phase interaction between mic signals, position the mid mic and the side mic in the closest proximity to each other possible.

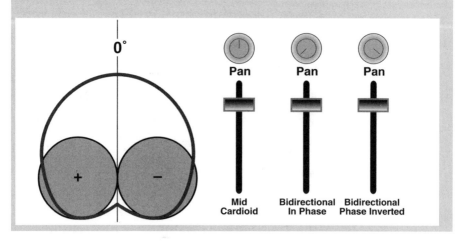

plays a very important part in the sound of any distant stereo mic setup.

It's also especially important when using stereo mic techniques that the instrument be in peak condition. Subtle nuances within the instrument's sound become more pronounced in these stereo configurations.

There are several standard stereo miking techniques that have been put to good practical use over the years. Some are very specific about the distances at which the mics should be separated as well as the polar patterns. Use these examples to develop configurations that you like and that capture the music in a way that feels good to you. We use many techniques in recording music, but always keep in mind that what we must continually focus on is the emotion of the music and whether we've captured it.

The Head

Another wonderful technique for stereo recording is called the binaural technique. This technique uses an actual synthetic head to house two very small condenser mic capsules. The capsules are placed inside the synthetic head, where the

Other Common Stereo Mic Techniques

These techniques offer more options for creative flexibility. They're quick and easy to set up once you're in the stereo miking mode.

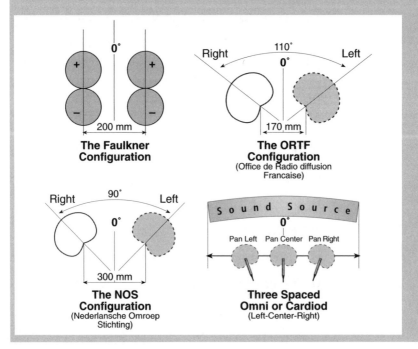

The Faulkner Configuration

The ORTF Configuration
(Office de Radio diffusion Francaise)

The NOS Configuration
(Nederlansche Omroep Stichting)

Three Spaced Omni or Cardiod
(Left-Center-Right)

eardrums of a real head would be. This synthetic head even has the ear flaps, or pinna.

Recordings made with the synthetic head—called a binaural mic—have incredible stereo imaging. When you listen to the recordings through headphones, sounds from all directions can be perceived. Sounds can be localized—their point of origin can be pinpointed—to be in front, behind, above, left, right or anywhere in between. The only drawback to the binaural technique is that the stereo imaging is drastically reduced when the recording is heard on regular monitors.

3:1 Principle

When setting up multi-mic recording situations, use this rule of thumb whenever possible: The distance between any two mics should be at least three times the distance from the mic to its intended source. This guideline aids you in placing microphones for minimal phase confusion when the mics are summed to mono—or to one track of the multitrack.

That simply means: If you have a microphone one foot from its source, there shouldn't be another mic closer than three feet to that microphone.

The 3:1 Principle

The distance between any two mics should be at least three times the distance from the mic to its intended source.

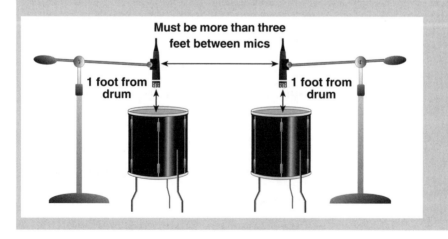

Must be more than three feet between mics

1 foot from drum

1 foot from drum

Amplified Electric Guitar

Now let's focus on the miked amplifier/ speaker cabinet sound. This is the most popular sound for recorded electric guitar. Guitarists typically think of their guitar amp as a unit that includes the speaker or speaker cabinet. Sometimes people try to literalize the concept of miking the amp to insinuate that you would actually place a mic in front of the power amplifier instead of the speaker. This is obviously not what is implied when someone asks you to mike the guitar amp. It's common to refer to miking the guitar amp, but it actually means to place a mic in front of the guitarist's speaker cabinet.

A guitar going through a direct box straight into the mixer usually sounds too harsh and sterile for most tastes. The guitar amp tends to smooth out the guitar sound so when we record the speaker of the amp, we usually get a sound that blends into the mix better than a direct sound.

When a guitarist chooses equipment, the selections are based almost totally on sound. The other factors to equipment selection are price and features, but I think we can agree that serious guitar players develop their distinct sounds largely through the equipment they choose. The guitar amplifier is one of the key factors in this sound scheme. We usually get the best and most usable sounds when we mic the amp. Different amplifiers have different sounds, especially when they distort.

Mic Choice and Position

Using a mic to capture the sound of the guitarist is not as simple as just selecting the best mic. Where we place the mic and where we place the amp can be equally influential on the final sound of the instrument. Although there are hundreds of different microphone available from many manufacturers, they essentially all fit into three basic categories: condenser, moving-coil and ribbon. Condenser and moving-coil mikes are the most common of these three, although they may all be used in recording as well as live situations.

It's ideal if you have at least one good moving-coil mic and one good condenser mic for your recordings. With these two options available you can cover most recording situations and achieve professional sounding results. Don't waste money on cheap mics unless you're buying them for artistic and sonic novelties. High-quality well-respected mics will last a long time and always provide usable sounds with sonic integrity.

The Most Common Approach
Turn the amp up to a fairly strong level. This doesn't have to be screaming loud, but most amps sound fuller if they're turned up a bit.

Next, place a moving-coil mic about one foot away from the speaker. Most guitar amps will have one or two full range speakers. These speakers are typically 8 to 12 inches in diameter. Moving-coil mics are the preferred choice for close-miking amplifiers because they can handle plenty of volume before they distort the sound. Also, the tone coloration of a moving-coil mic in the higher frequencies can add bite and clarity to the guitar sound.

If the amp you are miking has more than one identical speaker, point the mic at one of the speakers. Point the mic at the center of the speaker to get a sound with more bite and edge. Point the mic more toward the outer rim of the speaker to capture a warmer, smoother sound with less edge.

If you're miking a speaker enclosure with separate tweeter, midrange and bass speakers, you'll need to move the mic back two or three feet just to get the overall sound of the cabinet. This gets us into a situation where the room sound

Pointing the mic at the center of the speaker produces a sound with more high-frequency edge.

Pointing the mic away from the center of the speaker and toward the outer edge of the cone produces a warmer, smoother sound with less treble.

becomes an important part of the sound that goes onto the tape.

Audio Example 6 demonstrates the sound of an amp with the mic placed six inches from the speaker and pointed directly at the center of the speaker.

Audio Example 6
Mic at the Center of the Speaker

Audio Example 7 demonstrates the sound of the same amp, same guitar and same musical part as Audio Example 4-30.

Now the mic is aimed about one inch in from the outside rim of the speaker while maintaining the distance of six inches from the speaker.

Audio Example 7
Mic at the Outer Edge of the Speaker

When the mic is within a foot of the speaker, the room sound has minimal effect on the sound that goes to tape, especially if the amp volume is strong. If the guitarist hasn't already included reverb and delay in the selection of effects, this approach will give you consistently close-sounding tracks that you can add distance (ambience) to by adding reverb or delay in the mix.

Powerful guitar sounds often include the sound of the immediate space (the room) that the amp is in. This can be accomplished with reverb, but natural ambience can add an unusual and distinct quality to a recording. Try including the

Sound Advice on Microphone Techniques

sound of the room with the sound of the guitar. This technique often breathes life into an otherwise dull sound.

As we move the mic back more than a couple of feet from any amp, we're using distant miking. The room sound becomes part of the overall sound. We can get great guitar sounds if we put one mic within a foot of the amp and one mic back in the room several feet away from the amp. With this technique, we can blend the sound of the mic closest to the amp with ambient sound captured by the mic farther away. We can combine these two sounds to one track as we record, or if tracks permit, we can print each mic to a separate track and save the blending or panning for mix-down. The effectiveness of this approach is dependent on whether the sound of the room is musically appropriate.

Use a condenser mic to record the most accurate sound of the room. Condensers have a fuller sound from a distance than moving-coil or ribbon mics and they capture the subtleties of the room sound in more detail.

Acoustic Guitars

If I have an electric acoustic guitar should I mike it or run it through a direct box? Acoustic guitars with pickups can work well in a live performance situation. Simply plug into the board, an amp or through a direct box. You can get a passable sound and eliminate one microphone in the setup. However, though the sound can be okay for live performances it's hardly ever a great sound for recording. The sound from an electric acoustic pickup typically sounds sterile and small and it doesn't have the broad, full, interesting sound of the acoustic instrument. To run an electric acoustic guitar direct into a mixer, follow the same procedure as with any electric guitar.

Mic Choice

Typically, the best kind of mic to use on any acoustic guitar is a condenser mic. Condensers capture more of the subtlety of the attack, the sound of the pick on the strings and the nuance of artistic expression. Also, condenser microphones produce a full sound when miking from a distance. Moving-coil mics and ribbon mics can produce passable acoustic guitar sounds, especially if that's all you have, but the accepted mic of choice for acoustic guitars is a condenser.

The steel string acoustic is the most common acoustic guitar. These guitars come in many different shapes, sizes and brands. Each variation has a characteristic sound, but the primary trait of the acoustic guitar is a very clear and full sound. The second most common type of acoustic guitar is the nylon string classical guitar.

Bass Roll-Off

With a condenser mic six to eight inches from the guitar, we can potentially get a sound that has too much bass, especially as we move over the sound hole. We can control the frequency content of the acoustic guitar sound dramatically by changing mic placement. If there are too many lows in your acoustic guitar sound, try moving the mic up the neck and away from the sound hole, moving the mic back away from the guitar to the distance of one or two feet or turning the low frequencies down.

One way to turn the low frequencies down is by using the bass roll-off switch. Most condenser microphones have a switch to turn the bass frequencies down. These switches may have a number by them to indicate the frequency where the roll-off starts. The number is typically between 60 and 150. If there's no number, there might be a single line that slopes down to the left. When you use a condenser mic for close-miking, you'll usually need to use the bass roll-off switch to keep a good balance between lows and highs.

Aim the Mic

If we point a mic at different parts of the acoustic guitar while it's being played, we find that each zone has a different sound. There are all sorts of tricky ways to combine these different sounds from different places on the guitar, but it's usually best to keep it simple. More mics mean more chances of problematic phase interaction and more chance that your great stereo sound will turn to mush when your mix is heard in mono.

I've tried many techniques for miking acoustic guitars, using up to four or five mics. The method that consistently works the best for me uses one good condenser mic placed in the position that gets the sound I need for the track.

There are three common positions to mike the guitar: in front of the sound hole, behind the bridge and over the neck. Though each instrument has its own characteristic sound, each of these possible mic positions holds a consistent type of sound from one guitar to the next: Over the neck contains the highs, over the sound hole contains the lows and over the body behind the bridge contains the mids.

We'll use a steel string acoustic for the next set of Audio Examples, but all the techniques are worth trying on any acoustic steel string, nylon string or 12-string guitar.

If you position the mic directly over the sound hole, the sound will be bass-heavy and boomy like the sound in Audio Example 8.

Audio Example 8

The Sound Hole

If you position the mic over the top and behind the bridge, the sound will be strongest in mids like the sound in Audio Example 9.

Audio Example 9

Behind the Bridge

Point the mic at the front of the neck to hear more highs from the guitar, like the sound in Audio Example 10. This mic position can produce an excellent and usable sound, but you might have a problem with string and finger noise.

Audio Example 10

Over the Neck

The sound I get from one condenser mic pointed at the front of the neck, between the sound hole and where the neck joins the body of the guitar is very often the most usable. That doesn't mean that I don't use other techniques. Neither does it mean I'm not always trying new approaches on these instruments. In reality, we can do almost anything in almost any way and still get away with it if the sound supports the musical impact. Take these standard techniques and build on them. Push the limits.

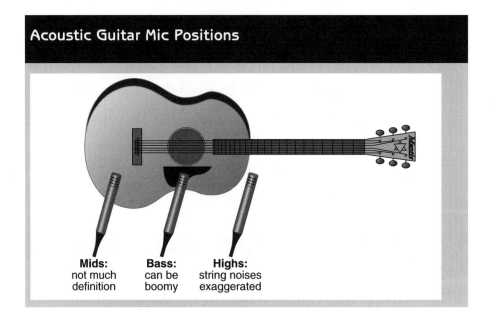

Acoustic Guitar Mic Positions

Mids:	Bass:	Highs:
not much	can be	string noises
definition	boomy	exaggerated

When we miked the electric guitar amp, the room began to play an important part in the sound of the instrument. The same is true for miking the acoustic. As we move the mic away from the instrument, the character of the sound changes dramatically. The music you're recording determines the usefulness of room sound.

Sound Advice on Microphone Techniques

Theories of Drum Miking

Most of the drum sounds you hear on albums are achieved through the use of several microphones recorded separately to several tracks that are blended and balanced during the mixdown. This is ideal. Practically speaking, most people don't have a pile of microphones to use at home, let alone 8 to 12 available tracks on the multitrack for drums. Most people have one or two microphones, and these microphones weren't purchased with drums or percussion in mind, but as your setup and skills build you'll want to build your arsenal of task-specific microphones.

You should have a good condenser mic for over the drum set and for cymbals. Condensers are the mic of choice for percussion, and they do the best job of capturing the true sound of each instrument. The fact that condenser microphones respond to transients more accurately than the other types of microphones makes them an obvious choice for percussion instruments, like tambourine, shaker, cymbals, triangle, claves or guiro.

The mic of choice for close-miking toms, snare and kick is a moving-coil mic, like a Shure SM57, Sennheiser 421 or Electro-Voice RE20. Though they don't have the transient response of condenser microphones, moving-coil microphones work great for close-miking drums because they can withstand intense amounts of volume before distorting. Also, most moving-coil microphones have a built-in sensitivity in the upper frequency range, which provides an EQ that accentuates the attack of the drum.

Most reasonably priced condenser and moving-coil microphones can give you good results. I don't recommend buying the least expensive mic, but you don't have to use a $3000 mic to achieve acceptable results either. Believe me, as you record more you'll start to have favorite microphones for each task. With all things in perspective, there are plenty of microphones available that can act as excellent tools for your recordings.

Recording a Kit With Four Mics

With four microphones on the set, you begin to have good control over the kick and snare sounds, plus you can get a stereo image. Some very acceptable drum sounds can be achieved using a setup with one kick mic, one snare mic, and two overheads. You'll need to experiment with placement of the microphones (especially the overheads), but solid and unique kick and snare drum sounds are possible with this mic technique. The individual microphones plus the overheads used in a stereo configuration can provide an excellent stereo image. The set in Audio Example 11 was miked with one kick mic, one snare mic and two overheads in an X-Y configuration.

Snare, Kick and X-Y

As we add microphones to our setup, we can either print each mic to a separate track on the multitrack, or we can do a sub-mix on the mixer, printing the entire kit to one or two tracks. It's ideal to keep as much flexibility as possible for the mix-down, but, if you're using a 4- or 8-track multitrack you'll probably only be able to justify allocating one or two tracks for the drums. Try recording the individual drum microphones on four to six tracks of an 8-track. Then bounce those tracks down to either a mono track or, in stereo, bounce them to two tracks.

As you consider different approaches to drum miking, it's important to note that no method is always the perfect choice. Part of the fun of recording is in the creative choices we can make musically and technically.

1. Two cardioid condenser microphones in a traditional X-Y configuration above the kit.

2. One cardioid moving-coil mic inside the kick.

3. One cardioid moving-coil mic from about 2" above the top head.

Adjust for the proper balance between the drums and cymbals

Close-mike Technique

The most common approach to getting good, punchy, drum sounds that have unique character is to use the close-mic technique. Each drum will typically have its own mic. Each of these microphones plus two overheads will be printed to separate tracks of the multitrack. These tracks will either stay separate until the mixdown, or they might be combined with the assignment buses and bounced to stereo tracks, making room for more instruments or voices.

If tracks are limited, the microphones can be combined through the mixer to one or two tracks of the multitrack on the initial recording. Simply separately record the kick drum, snare drum, two separate tom microphones and two separate overheads to tracks one through six of the 8-track multitrack. Next, assign playback of those tracks to tracks seven and eight of the multitrack with the channel assign bus. With this setup you can re-equalize each track to obtain the optimum sound quality, add effects to individual drums and blend the drum mix for each musical section. If we want to put a lot of gated reverb on the toms but not on the kick or snare, we can do it using the close mic

Sound Advice on Microphone Techniques

approach. We have flexibility that isn't possible using one or two microphones. If you're bouncing multiple tracks down to a stereo pair, use the pan controls to set up a stereo mix of the entire kit.

It's possible to use up a lot of tracks once you begin close-miking drums. Most projects using 24 tracks or more can justify allotting 8 to 16 tracks just for the drum set. This isn't an option for most people in their home studios, but be aware that the more isolation you can get, the more precisely you'll be able to shape each sound. There are even plenty of ways to expand on this approach. Try including room ambience microphones, a mic under the snare, individual cymbal microphones or any creative new approach you can dream up.

The drum set in Audio Example 12 is set up with one kick mic, one snare mic, one mic on each tom, two microphones overhead in an X-Y pattern and one hi-hat mic.

1. *Two cardioid condenser microphones in a traditional X-Y configuration above the kit.*
2. *One cardioid moving-coil mic inside the kick.*
3. *One cardioid moving-coil mic about 2" above the top head.*
4. *One cardioid moving-coil mic pointed at the floor tom.*
5. *One cardioid moving-coil mic aimed between the upper two toms and positioned so that the two drums are balanced and blended.*

Adjust for the proper balance between the drums and cymbals

Audio Example 12
Snare, Kick, Toms and X-Y

Recording Vocals

The art of vocal recording is very involved. It's amazing how sensitive, both mentally and physically, the vocal instrument is. Singing is an interesting blend of technical ability, physical talent and emotional interpretation. There must be a good balance between these factors.

Vocals are the focal point of almost all commercial songs. If the vocals sound good, the song will probably sound good. If they sound bad, the song will probably sound bad. The vocal tracks typically contain the most apparent emotional content and impact of the song. Most listeners focus on the vocals first.

Mic Placement

Placement of the microphone in relation to the singer is a key variable. Not only does it matter where the mic is, but the best placement changes depending on the type of mic you're using, the vocal timbre, musical style and personal taste.

Condenser microphones are usually the first choice for studio vocal applications. Commercial vocal sounds vary, but most professionally recorded hit vocals are recorded with a good condenser mic set on cardioid pickup pattern, from a distance of 6 to 12 inches. A vocal that's recorded at this distance sounds full and warm on most condenser mics. Recording at this proximity provides the recordist with the option of including the inherent sound of the acoustical environment in varying degrees. Most lead vocals blend better in the mix when recorded with the microphone about a foot or so from the vocalist. Close-mike technique (from a distance of one to three inches) typically provides a sound that is a little too thick and cumbersome, especially when using a condenser mic.

If you're using a moving-coil mic, vocals sound thin and tinny from distances greater than six to eight inches. If you only have a moving-coil mic, you'll get the best results when close-miking solo vocals. When miking group vocals with a moving-coil mic, some fairly extreme addition of low-end EQ, or subtraction of the appropriate high-frequency, might be necessary to fill out the sound.

It's clear that the room and mic distance play an important part in the sound of the vocal. We need a good set of rules about recording vocals to help provide a starting point for our choice of recording technique. Don't feel bound by these rules—many great vocal sounds have been recorded through techniques that break the rules—but use them as a foundation for your choices. Let's consider mics in two categories:

1. Moving-coil and ribbon
2. Condenser

Moving-coil/Ribbon

Moving-coil and ribbon mics are almost always designed for close-miking applications and don't typically provide a full sound when the singer is more than six to eight inches from the mic. To get a full, natural sound from these mics, it's best to record the singer from a distance of two to six inches. Moving-coil mics and ribbon mics are the standard choice for live sound reinforcement applications because they work best at close range. In addition, moving-coil microphones are well-suited to live sound reinforcement use because they are the most durable of all the common mic types. Ribbon mics aren't very durable but they provide a good sound when close-miking vocals.

Condenser

When recording vocals in a recording studio, condenser microphones are almost always the best choice. The condenser mic operating principle is best suited to accurately capture a singer's natural sound because they color the sound less than other mic types. They also respond more accurately to transients, therefore producing a vocal sound that's very natural and understandable.

Unlike moving-coil and ribbon mics, condenser microphones sound full from a distance of one or two feet. The singer can stand back from the mic a bit and you can still record a full, present sound while retaining the option to include more or less of the room's acoustical character. Miking vocals from one or two feet away often produces a unique and transparent sound. Sometimes when vocals are close-miked, especially with condenser microphones, they sound boomy and thick and don't blend well with the rest of the mix. The vocal line in Audio Example 13 was recorded with a condenser mic from about six inches.

Audio Example 13
Vocal Melody From Six Inches (Condenser)

Audio Example 14 demonstrates the same vocal line as Audio Example 13, this time recorded from a distance of about 12 inches. Notice that the line still sounds full.

Audio Example 14
Vocal Melody From 12 Inches (Condenser)

The condenser mic capsule doesn't respond well to moisture. If the singer is too close, the mic might suddenly quit working and remain inoperable until the capsule dries out. When the capsule dries off sufficiently the mic will work again, but it's frustrating when this happens. If you want the close-miked sound from a condenser mic, use a foam wind screen to diffuse as much air and moisture as possible.

Stylistic Considerations

Usually in commercial popular music it's best to record vocals in a room that's acoustically neutral (doesn't have a long reverberation time) and mike the vocalist from a distance of 6 to 12 inches. This approach provides the most flexibility during mixdown. You maintain the freedom to use reverberation and other effects to artificially place the vocal in the space that best suits the emotion of the music.

For classically oriented vocal recordings, it's often the technique of choice to find a great-sounding room or concert hall, then mike the singer from a distance that includes the desired amount of room sound. The room sound is all-important to this vocal-recording approach, and it's common for the best classical singers to travel anywhere in the world to sing a piece of music in the concert hall that they feel is best for the music.

Even for commercial pop styles, you should be willing to experiment with different uses of ambience. Mainly, take care that you don't include so much ambience that the vocal loses the close intimacy that sounds good on a lot of popular music.

Wind Screen

A wind screen is used in the studio to keep abundant air, caused by hard enunciation, from creating loud pops as the microphone capsule is overworked. In an outdoor application, the wind screen is also used to shield the capsule from wind.

Most vocal recordings require the use of a wind screen, also called a pop filter. When a singer pronounces words containing hard consonants, like "p" and "b," there's a lot of air hitting the mic capsule at once. When the air from these hard consonants, called plosives, hits the mic capsule, it can actually bottom out the capsule diaphragm. In other words, this "pop" can be the physical sound of the microphone diaphragm actually hitting the end of its normal travel range. On our recorder, we hear this as a loud and obvious pop.

Sound Advice on Microphone Techniques

The Foam Wind Screen

There are many different types and shapes of foam wind screens. They work very well when used in the proper context but can adversely affect sound quality.

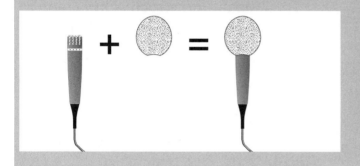

A wind screen can diffuse the air from the singer before it gets to the mic capsule, therefore eliminating the problem plosive. Wind screens come in many different forms. Moving-coil and ribbon mics often have the wind screen built in. Most condenser mics don't have the wind screen built in. Since the condenser microphones sound full from a distance, we can have the singer stand back far enough that plosives aren't much of a problem, and we'll still get a full, natural sound. Depending on the singer and the sound you want, you might not be able to keep the mic far enough away to avoid plosives while still achieving the sound you want.

Try a foam wind screen. They come in different shapes, sizes and colors, but they're all made from molded porous foam. Their purpose is to diffuse the air before it reaches the mic capsule. Foam wind screens are the typical choice for outdoor applications because they surround the mic capsule completely and offer the most complete wind diffusion. Purists often reject foam wind screens for any use other than outdoor applications because they muffle the sound and attenuate the high frequencies more than the other designs.

Another type of wind screen can be constructed from a piece of an old panty hose, an embroidery hoop and a mic clip. This design works very well, is inexpensive and typically sounds much better than foam. The nylon, stretched over the hoop and placed between the singer's mouth and the microphone, usually diffuses the air enough to avoid plosives and muffles the sound less than a foam wind screen.

Embroidery Hoop Wind Screen

This wind screen uses a piece of a nylon stocking stretched over an embroidery hoop and attached to the bottom part of a standard mic clip. Most embroidery hoops fit very nicely in the mic clip that comes with a Shure SM57 or SM58. Mount this device on a separate mic stand and place it front of the mic between the singer and the microphone diaphragm.

Piano Mic Techniques

Before you start miking any piano, see that it's in tune and has been serviced to eliminate buzzes, clicks and thumps. If there are physical noises that occur spontaneously while the piano plays, your job is suddenly much more difficult than it should be. The piano must sound good by itself so that it will meet the high standards you should be setting for your recordings.

The Basics

Whether recording a nine-foot grand piano, a spinet piano, an old-time upright piano or a sampled piano, it's understood that we're trying to achieve the full, rich sound that only an acoustic piano can provide. A great piano, miked and recorded well, has life, transparency and openness that's hard to beat.

Grand Piano

In Audio Example 15, listen to a grand piano miked with a couple of good condenser mics for a wide, impressive solo piano sound.

Audio Example 15

Stereo Grand Piano

The method of choice for most engineers when recording grand piano is two good condenser mics aimed at the strings. One mic is placed over the high strings, and the other over the low strings. When these mics are panned across the stereo spectrum, the piano has a very big sound and provides good support for most vocal or instrumental solos. How far apart you pan the highs and lows is dependent on the musical context: If the two mics can be printed to separate tracks of the multitrack, save these pan decisions for mixdown.

Stereo Grand Piano

Two condenser mics are aimed at the strings from above the piano with the lid open on the long or short stick. Mic 1 is centered over the treble strings, 6–18" above the strings and 6–18" behind the hammers. Mic 2 is centered over the bass strings, 6–18" from the strings and 2–4' from the end of the piano, depending on the size of the piano and the desired sound.

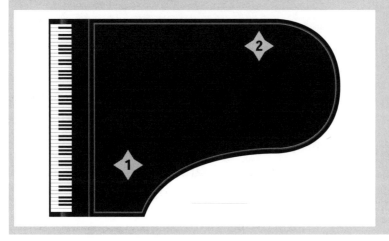

In order to get a good transition from lows to highs and a good recording of most of the piano range, it's necessary to keep the mics about a foot or more from the strings. If the mics are placed much closer, the mid notes might get lost in the blend. This can sometimes be at the expense of the very highs and the very lows, but that's OK if you're getting the sound that supports the music or the piano part doesn't use the extreme highs and lows of the keyboard.

Always experiment with the exact mic placement for two specific reasons:

- Different musical parts have different musical ranges for the left and/or the right hand. Musical style and consideration dictate the microphone placement.

- Again, the phase interaction between the two microphones is critical. If the distance between the mics changes a few inches, the sound of the piano changes drastically when heard in mono.

There are quite a few variables involved with piano so let's look at some of the differences in sound that we can bring about with the various techniques we apply.

Mics Close to the Strings and Each Other

If mics 1 and 2 are close to the strings, they need to be close to each other to fill in the mid notes. This decreases the punch of the very high and very low notes, but it produces a close sound that's quite good. Be sure you check the sound of the two mics summed to mono before you record the piano track.

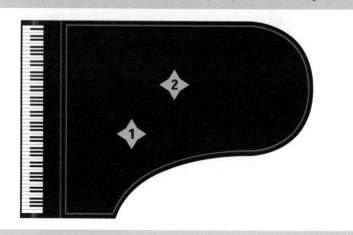

The intensity of the transient is dependent upon the condition of the felt hammers and the brilliance of the strings. The felt hammers on any piano can be conditioned to produce a sharper attack with a brighter tone or a duller attack with a mellower tone. If you have the felt hammers on your piano conditioned, keep in mind that a brighter sound with more attack stands out in a rhythm section mix very well; on the other hand, solo pianists often prefer a darker, mellower tone. This conditioning is called voicing the piano.

The grand piano in Audio Example 16 is miked with one condenser mic inside the wide open lid, from a distance of about three feet. It's necessary to keep the mic back a little to get an even balance between the low notes and the high notes.

Audio Example 16
One Condenser Mic From Three Feet

Mic Choice

Each condenser microphone provides a unique sound on piano. Even though two mics might have identical specifications, the sounds they produce might be very different. Here are some mics that I've used on grand piano and some of my observations on them. Keep in mind that each room and each piano is a little different.

Miking the Piano With One Condenser

With the lid wide open, place one condenser mic centered at the opening of the lid. Position the mic for the sound that provides the best musical support.

Most of us have a limited number of choices when it comes to mic selection. If all you own is a moving-coil mic like the SM57, then that's what you'll need to use. But as your engineering skills and opportunities increase, try any mic you can get your hands on. Even though high-quality condensers are typically preferred, each mic offers a unique sense of distance and tonal character.

Sound Advice on Microphone Techniques

Moving away from the piano provides an interesting texture, depending on the room where the piano is being recorded. It's usually best to mike the grand piano from within four feet of the sound board. Close-mike technique gives us an intimate sound that we can add space to with reverb if it's needed in the mix.

Room sound is easy to add with a good controllable reverb, but if the piano on tape has too much room sound, it's difficult or impossible to get rid of. The piano in Audio Example 17 is miked with a condenser microphone about six feet from the open piano lid. Notice the room sound.

Audio Example 17
One Mic Six Feet From the Open Piano Lid

When miking the piano with two mics, move in closer to the strings still enabling balance control between the treble and bass strings. With two mics, we can get as close as six inches from the strings. A distance of eight to twelve inches is usually the best for miking the grand piano with two mics.

Listen to the piano in Audio Example 18 miked with two condenser mics. First I solo the mic for the bass strings, then I solo the mic for the treble strings. Listen as I blend the two mics for a good even mono sound, then pan the two mics slowly apart for a wider stereo image.

Audio Example 18
Two Condenser Mics From About Eight Inches

There are several options for mic placement when miking the grand piano. The mics can either both be placed by the hammers, or they can be positioned with one mic over the treble strings by the hammers and the other over the bass strings, about halfway toward the far end of the piano.

In Audio Example 19, the piano is miked with two condenser mics a few inches behind the hammers: one aimed toward the high notes and one aimed toward the low notes. The mics are about a foot apart and about eight inches from the strings.

Audio Example 19
Two Condenser Mics by the Hammers

To get a wider stereo image, or to gain better control of the lows in relation to the highs, move the mics further apart. Compare Audio Example 20 to the previous example. Notice the difference in treble to bass balance with the mics further apart in example 5-7.

Audio Example 20
Two Condenser Mics Further Apart

Try miking the grand piano with a coincident stereo miking technique. Set up an X-Y mic configuration with the piano lid up and the mics facing toward the strings. Audio Example 21 demonstrates

the sound of a grand piano with two cardioid condenser mics placed at the edge
of the open piano facing in and positioned
in an X-Y configuration.

Both Mics by the Hammers

*Place both mics 6–12" behind the hammers, from a distance of 6–18". Center
mic 1 over the treble strings and center mic 2 over the bass strings.*

Audio Example 21
X-Y Configuration

Stereo or Mono

Even when the piano is miked with two mics, it's not always best to keep the piano stereo in the mix. If the stereo tracks are hard-panned, the sound might be unnatural, with the highs and lows spread far apart in the stereo image. Often the two mics—or tracks—are simply used to get a good balance between the treble, mid and bass strings. A mono track might sound very natural.

If the piano remains stereo, the mics might be soft-panned at about 10:00 and 2:00. If the piano is in the same rhythm section with a guitar, the stereo piano tracks often lean to one side—say at about 11:00 and 4:00—and the guitar track or tracks are positioned across the panorama to offset the piano.

Coincident Stereo Miking (X-Y)

Mics 1 and 2 are in a traditional X-Y configuration, facing into the piano at the edge with the lid open. This technique produces a full stereo sound with minimal problematic phase cancellation in mono.

Setting the Mood—Conclusion

In every situation, verify that the sound you're recording has integrity. Is the instrument in tune and at its peak condition? Does the vocalist sound good when it's time to track? Are the drumheads shot? If these types of details aren't covered you'll have a difficult time getting a really great recording.

Creating a comfortable, pleasant atmosphere for the pianist is an important part of a good recording, especially when recording a very emotional solo piece. The room temperature should be comfortable, and your attitude should be positive and supportive.

If these seem like unimportant factors to you, you're wrong. Recording music is an emotional experience for both the artist and the engineer. A negative attitude can destroy the emotion of a session and therefore destroy the interpretation of the music. Too many engineers, producers and musicians get so into the technical aspects of the recording process that they inhibit the artistic flow of the music. Somewhere between perfected details and totally free interpretation, there's a balance where the technical and emotional sides of the music are as good as they can cumulatively be for a particular moment in time.

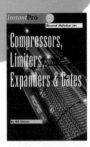

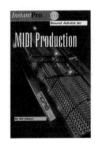